The Incredible Bible Stories

Volume 1

Mrs. Selvi Piyatina

Profile

The Incredible Bible Stories - Volume 1 is a collection of ten engaging and inspiring stories from the Old Testament. These stories cover the creation of the world, the story of Noah and the flood, Abraham's sacrifice of Isaac, Isaac meeting his wife Rebekah, Esau selling his birthright to Jacob, Jacob's acquired wealth in Padnaram, Jacob's mourning for Joseph, Joseph the overseer in Egypt, Joseph's dream come true and Jacob reunites with son Joseph.

The book is perfect for children and families who want to learn more about the stories from the Old Testament. The stories offer valuable lessons on faith, trust, obedience, and perseverance, making it a great resource for parents and teachers looking to instill these values in children.

Mrs. Selvi Piyaina MBA

Dedication

This book is dedicated to my beloved father, late S. P Anthony Cruze, who served his country as a wounded veteran of the Indian Army. His sacrifices and courage inspired me to pursue my dreams and never give up, even in the face of adversity. He instilled and taught me the importance of perseverance and hard work.

I also dedicate this book to my mother, who stood by my father's side as a pillar of support and strength, and who continued to be my guiding light after he passed away. Her unwavering love and encouragement gave me the courage to follow my passion and pursue my dreams.

To my parents, I owe everything. This book is a tribute to their unwavering love and support, and to the values they instilled in me. Thank you for everything, Mom and Dad.

Acknowledgements

My sincere gratitude goes to the Almighty for providing me with the knowledge and inspiration to write this book. It wouldn't have been possible without His guidance.

I also want to express my thanks to my husband, Dr. G. Rajendran, and my son, Mr. Jasper Sheleph, for their constant support and assistance throughout the entire process. Special thanks to Pastor T Durairaj for his supervision.

Lastly, I want to thank the readers of "Incredible Bible Stories". Your time and support are much appreciated, and I hope that this book inspires, educates, and captivating you."

The Incredible Bible Stories

Volume 1

Contents

from GENESIS CHAPTER 1 TO GENESIS CHAPTER 50:

1. THE CREATION

In the beginning, there was God. The earth was without form; it was void, and darkness was upon the face of the earth. The spirit of God moved upon the face of the waters, and God thought, "Let something happen".

"Let there be light," God said, and there was light. God saw that it was good and divided the light from the darkness. The light he called day, and the darkness he called night. The evening and the morning were the first day.

God said, "Let there be firmament" *(consisting of clouds, the sun, moon, stars, and planets)* amid the waters, and let it divide the waters from the waters. He called the firmament heaven and filled it with clouds. The evening and the morning were the second day.

The waters were gathered in one place, and they were called seas; and the dry land appeared, which was called the earth. The earth was filled with oceans, lakes, ponds, rivers, beaches, mountains, rocks, and small and big islands. Then God said let the earth bring forth fruit-bearing trees, whose seed is in itself. The fruits were of different sizes, colours, and tastes. There were also grass, bushes, and plants. The flowers and leaves of trees and plants were of different colours, and smells. The evening and the morning were the third day.

God wanted to separate the day from the night with different lights. He made two great lights. The greater light to rule the day, which is the sun, and the lesser light to rule the night, which is the moon that separated the light from the darkness. A special touch was given to the sky with billions of twinkling stars that appeared in the night. God saw that it was good. The evening and the morning were the fourth day.

On the fifth day, God created beautiful creatures to live in this world that has life. The winged birds that fly above the earth are of different sizes and colours, and made different sounds. The seas, oceans, rivers, and ponds were filled with swimming creatures like great whales, varieties of fish, and other amazing small creatures. God saw that it was good. He blessed the birds to be fruitful and multiply on the earth, and the swimming creatures to multiply in the waters.

God said let the earth bring forth living creatures, the animals like cattle, beasts, and creeping things. The beasts were like lions, tigers, elephants, bears, etc. Cattle like cows, dogs, cats, and creepy things like serpents, lizards, and so on. They were distinguished by their size and sound. Some of the animals were fierce, like the lion and the tiger.

Then God decided to create something special, and that was man. There was not a man to till the ground. God made man, and he created him in his own image to have domain (*control*) over all that he had created. God formed man from the dust of the ground and breathed into his nostrils the breath of life. Then man became a living soul, and called him Adam. Man had dominion over the beasts, cattle, creeping creatures of the earth, fowls of the air, and creatures of the water.

God said, I have given you every seed-bearing herb and every tree yielding fruit that has seed in it for you to eat. To the beasts of the earth, fowls of the air, and creeping creatures of the earth, God gave every green herb to eat. The Lord had not caused it to rain upon the earth. Only a mist went up from the earth and watered the whole face of the ground. God saw that all he had done was good. The evening and the morning were the sixth day. Thus, the heavens and the earth, as well as their hosts, were completed. On the seventh day, God ended all his work and rested. God blessed and sanctified (*made holy*) the seventh day.

Lord God planted a garden in the eastward, in Eden, and there he put the man whom he had formed to dress it and take care of it. Out of the ground grew every tree that was pleasant to the eyes and good for food. In the midst of the garden was the tree of life, which was called the tree of knowledge of good and evil. God commanded the man he created that he shall freely eat the fruit of all the trees in the garden except the tree of knowledge. The day you eat the fruit of knowledge, you will surely die.

A river went out of Eden to water the garden, which parted and became four heads. The name of the first river was Pison, where there was gold; the second river was Gihon, surrounding the whole land of Ethiopia. The third river was called Hiddekel, flowing towards Assyria, and the fourth river was the Euphrates.

God brought all the beasts, fowl of the air, and living beings of water that he formed out of the ground to Adam to name them all. Adam named all the beasts of the field, fowls of the air, creeping creatures, and living beings of water, that is called till today.

The Lord said that it was not good for a man to be alone and decided to make a companion for him. Then God caused a deep sleep to fall upon Adam, and he slept. God took one of Adam's ribs and closed that place with flesh instead. The rib that God took from Adam, he made a woman and brought her to the man. Then Adam said, since she is his bone and his flesh, she shall be called a woman, because she was taken out of the man. Adam called the woman "his wife, Eve, because she was the mother of all living." God said that the man should be fruitful, multiply, replenish, have control over, and have domain over, all the living things of the water and earth.

Among all the beasts that God had made, the serpent (*a snake*) was cunning. The serpent said to the woman, "Did God say unto you that you shall not eat of every fruit of the tree in the garden?" Then the woman said to the serpent, "God told us that we may eat all the fruit of the trees except the fruit of the tree that is in the middle of the garden." God told us not to eat its fruit or touch it because we would die. But the serpent told the woman, "You will not die. God knows that the day you eat that fruit, your eyes shall be opened, you will know the difference between good and evil, and you will be like God."

The woman saw that the fruit was good and pleasant to the eyes, which will make one wise. She ate the fruit and gave it to her husband, who also ate the fruit. Their eyes opened, and they knew that they were naked. Then they sewed the leaves of a fig tree together and made themselves aprons.

During the day when it was pleasant and cool, they heard the voice of the Lord God walking in the garden. Immediately Adam and his wife hid themselves among the trees of the garden. Then God called Adam and asked, "Where are you?" Adam said, I heard your voice, Lord, but I was afraid because I was naked, and I hid myself. God asked Adam, who told you that you were naked, "Did you eat the fruit which I told you not to eat?" Adam told God, "The woman whom you had given me gave me to eat, and I ate."

God asked the woman, "Why did you do this?" The woman said, "The serpent beguiled (*deceived*) me into eating the fruit, and I ate". Then the Lord said to the serpent, "Because you did this, you are cursed among all cattle and beasts." You will move on your belly and eat dust all the days of your life. I will put enmity between your seed and the woman. You will bruise their heel, and they will bruise your head.

God said to the woman, I will multiply your sorrow and conception greatly. In sorrow, you will bear children, and your husband will rule over you. To Adam, God said, because you heard your wife's voice and ate the fruit of the tree, that I commanded you not to eat, cursed be the ground for your sake. Thorns and thistles shall it bring, and in the sweat of your face you shall eat bread, till you return to the ground. For out of dust you came, and to dust you will return. God made coats out of skins and clothed Adam and Eve and sent them out of the Eden Garden to till the ground. God placed Cherubim's (*Angels*) and a flaming sword in Eden Garden, which turned every way.

Then Adam and his wife Eve left Eden Garden. God blessed Eve with a child, who was named Cain. She gave birth to another child, and they called him Abel. Cain used to till the ground, but Abel took care of the sheep. Cain brought the fruit of the ground as an offering to the Lord, and Abel brought home the firstlings of his flock as an offering. The Lord had respect for Abel and his offering, but God did not have respect for Cain's offering, and Cain was angry. Then the Lord asked Cain, "Why are you angry and sad?" God said you do good, and you will be accepted, and your brother will desire you. If not, sin will lie at your door when you do evil, and your brother will rule over him.

One day, when Cain and Abel were in the field, talking to each other, Cain rose against Abel, his brother, and slew him. The Lord asked Cain, "Where is your brother Abel?" Then Cain told God, I do not know; am I my brother's keeper? God said to Cain, "What have you done? The voice of your brother's blood is crying unto me from the ground." So now you are cursed by the earth, and henceforth, when you till the ground, it shall not give you a yield. You will be a fugitive and a vagabond on earth. Then Cain said unto the Lord, "The punishment is greater than I can bear." You have driven me this day from the face of the earth, and I must hide my face from you; anyone who finds me will slay me. The Lord said whoever slays Cain, revenge shall be taken on him sevenfold. Then the

Lord set a mark on Cain, that anyone who finds him should not kill him. Eventually, Cain went out from the presence of the Lord and dwelt in the land of Nod, in the east of Eden.

Adam and Eve had another son, and they called him Seth. Eve said the Lord had given Seth in place of Abel. Adam had sons and daughters after Seth. Adam lived for nine hundred and thirty years and then died.

2. NOAH'S ARK

Seth's great-grandson Enoch walked with God. He was taken by God when he was three hundred and sixty-five years old. All the days of Seth were nine hundred and twelve years. Enoch's son Methuselah had a son at the age of one hundred and eighty-seven years, whose name was Lamech. When Lamech was one hundred and eighty-two years old, he had a son and named him Noah. Methuselah lived nine hundred and sixty-nine years; Lamech lived seven hundred and seventy-seven years and died. Methuselah is the oldest man on earth.

God saw that the wickedness of man was great on earth and that every imagination of the thoughts of men was only evil. He repented and grieved for having put man on the face of the earth. The Lord decided to destroy man, whom he created. He also wanted to destroy the beasts, creeping things, and fouls of the air. But among all these, Noah, a just and perfect man of his generation, walked with God and found grace in the eyes of the Lord. Noah had three sons: Shem, Ham, and Japheth.

God told Noah that the earth is filled with violence and people are corrupted, and he would like to destroy them along with the earth. He told Noah to make an Ark of gopher wood with a lot of rooms. God gave the prescriptions to build the Ark. The Ark was 300 cubits long (*one cubit is 20.2 inches wide*), 50 cubits wide, and 30 cubits tall. The Ark had three stories: a lower deck, a middle deck, and an upper deck. The Ark had one window and a door and was covered inside and out with pitch (*a sticky substance*).

God told Noah he would bring a flood upon the earth to destroy all the flesh under the heavens and that everything on the earth would die, but with you, I would establish a binding agreement. You shall go into the Ark with your wife, your three sons, and your three son's wives.

Noah was asked to bring into the Ark two of every living creature, from fowls of the air to cattle, beasts, water animals, and creeping things, to keep them alive. They shall be male and female. God commanded Noah to store sufficient food for his family and for the other living creatures with him in the Ark. God told Noah to take seven of every clean beast, male and female, and two of every unclean beast, male and female. Of fowls of the air, also seven, male and female, to keep them alive upon the face of the earth.

God told Noah that in seven days he would cause rain to fall upon the earth for forty days and forty nights. I will destroy every living substance that I have made from the earth. Noah had completed all that God had commanded him to do. Noah was six hundred years old when the flood of waters came upon the earth.

Noah went into the Ark with his wife, his three sons, Shem, Ham, and Japheth, and their wives. Likewise, all the beasts, cattle, fowl of the air, creeping things, and water animals went into the Ark. Then the Lord shut them in. When Noah was six hundred years old, on the seventeenth day of the second month, the windows of heaven were opened. The rain was upon the earth for forty days and forty nights. The waters increased, and the Ark was lifted above the earth. The earth was filled with water, and all the high hills and mountains were covered with it. The Ark was lifted above the earth and floated.

All the flesh that moved upon the earth died, including every man, the beasts, the cattle, the fowls of the air, and the creeping things. Only Noah, his family of eight, and the animals and fowl that went into the Ark remained alive. The water prevailed upon the earth for one hundred and fifty days.

God remembered Noah and all the living things inside the Ark. God made a wind to pass over the earth to make the lashing water quiet. After one hundred and fifty days, the water started subsiding. On the seventh month and the seventeenth day, the Ark rested upon the mountain of Ararat. The water level decreased continuously until the tenth month.

On the first day of the tenth month, the tops of the mountains were seen. After forty days, Noah opened the window of the Ark that he had made and sent forth a raven. The raven went to-and-fro until the water dried from the earth. He also sent a dove to see if the water had abated (*reduced*). But the dove did not find a place to rest her foot, and she returned to Noah in the Ark because the water was still there on the face of the earth. Then Noah put forth his hand and pulled the dove inside the Ark.

After seven days, Noah sent the dove out of the Ark. The dove came back to him in the evening with an olive leaf in her mouth. Noah knew that the water on the earth had decreased. Yet, after another seven days, he sent forth the dove, which did not return.

In the year six hundred and one, in the first month and the first day, the water dried up on the earth. Noah removed the covering of the Ark and looked out, and he found that the ground was dry. In the second month, on the twenty-seventh day, the earth was fully dried up. God told Noah to leave the Ark with his wife, his three sons, and their wives. He told Noah to bring all the beasts, cattle, fowl of the air, creeping things, and water animals out of the Ark so that they would be fruitful and multiply upon the earth.

Then the Lord decided that he would not curse the ground again for man's sake and would not kill every living thing. As long as the earth remains, the seasons of seedtime and harvest, cold and heat, summer and winter, day and night, shall not cease. God blessed Noah and his sons to be fruitful, multiply abundantly, and replenish the earth.

God told Noah that every moving thing that lives shall be meat for you, but do not eat the blood of the flesh; you can consume the green herb as well. God established a covenant with Noah and his seed. When a bow appears in the cloud, I will remember my covenant, not to destroy all flesh by the waters. Noah lived for three hundred and fifty years after the flood and gave up the ghost at the age of nine hundred and fifty years.

3. ABRAHAM SACRIFICES ISAAC

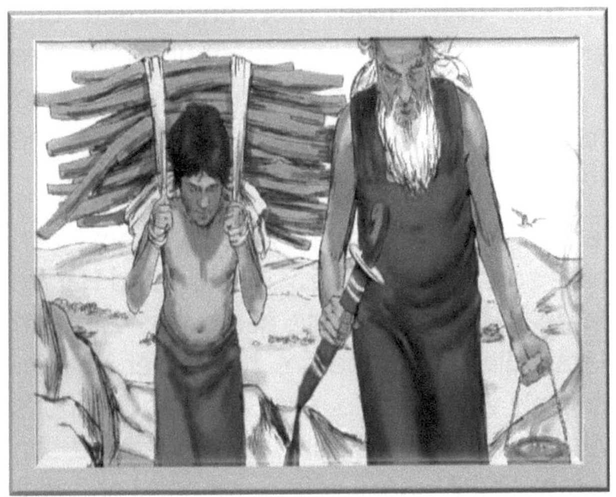

God blessed and multiplied Noah's family abundantly. The whole earth spoke one language. The people then decided to build a city and a tower to create a name for themselves, the top of which could reach the heavens, so that they would not be scattered. Lord came down to see the city and the tower and confounded (*confused*) their languages so that they might not understand one another's. Lord scattered them upon the face of all the earth as per their language, and they left off to build the city. As a result, the city was given the name Babel.

Terah, the great-grandson of Shem, had three sons named Abram, Nahor, and Haran. Haran had a son whose name was Lot, and Haran died in Ur before his father, Terah. Abram's wife's name was Sarai, and Nahor's wife was Milcah. Terah, along with his son Abram and Abram's wife Sarai and Lot, went into the land of Canaan and dwelt in Haran. Terah died in Haran when he was two hundred and five years old.

The Lord told Abram to depart out of Haran. So, Abram took Sarai, his wife, and Lot, with all their substance and all the souls they had in Haran, and they went to the land of

Canaan and then to Egypt. The Lord appeared unto Abram and said, "Unto your seed I will give this land."

Abram was very rich in cattle, silver, and gold. Lot was also blessed with flocks, herds, and tents. The land was not able to bear both, for their substance was so great that they could not dwell together. In the meantime, there was a strife (*conflict*) between the herdsmen of Abram's cattle and the herdsmen of Lot's cattle. So Abram said to Lot, "The whole land is before you." If you go to the left, then I will go to the right; if you go to the right, then I will go to the left. Then Lot lifted up his eyes and chose the plain of Jordan, which was well watered everywhere, and they separated themselves one from the other. Abram dwelled in the land of Canaan, and Lot dwelled towards Sodom.

Then the Lord said unto Abram, "Look from the place where you are," northward, southward, eastward, and westward; all the land that you see, I will give it to you and your seed forever. I will make your seed like the dust of the earth; if a man can number the dust of the earth, then your seed also can be numbered. Then Abram said, Lord, my wife Sarai bore me no children. There is no heir after me; I am childless. Then the Lord brought Abram out and said, "Look towards heaven and tell me; if you can count the stars," so shall be thy seed. Abram believed in God.

When Abram was ninety-nine years old, the Lord appeared unto him and said, I am the Almighty God; walk before me and be perfect. I will make an agreement between myself and you and will multiply you exceedingly. Then Abram fell on his face and worshipped God. Then God said you shall be a father of many nations. Henceforth your name shall not be called Abram but shall be called Abraham. God said I will give you and your generation the land wherein you are a stranger. I will give all the land of Canaan as an everlasting possession, and I will be their

God. Your wife, Sarai, shall henceforth be called Sarah.

I will bless Sarah and give you a son, and she shall be a mother of nations; kings shall be born through her. Then Abraham fell on his face and laughed, and he said in his heart, "Shall a child be born unto me when I am one hundred years old and my wife Sarah is ninety years old?" Then God said, Sarah, your wife, shall bear a son next year at the same time, and you will call his name Isaac. I will establish an everlasting bond with him and with his generation after him.

The Lord appeared to Abraham on the plains of Mamre while he was sitting in the tent door in the heat of the day. When Abraham looked up, three men stood by him. When he saw them, he ran to meet them from the tent door and bowed himself towards the ground. He told them that if I have found favour, please do not go away. I will fetch some water, wash your feet, and rest yourselves under the tree. I will bring some bread; you can have it and go your way. The men agreed.

Then Abraham ran into the tent and told Sarah to make some bread. In the meantime, Abraham fetched a tender and good calf and gave it to his servant to dress and cook. Then he took butter, milk, bread, and the cooked meat and set it before the three men, and he stood by them under the tree, and the three men did eat.

Then they asked, "Where is your wife, Sarah?" Abraham said that she is in the tent. One of the men said, "When I return next time, your wife Sarah shall have a son. Sarah was standing behind the tent door and heard this. Hearing this, Sarah laughed to herself, saying, I am old, and my husband is also old. And the Lord said to Abraham, "Why did Sarah laugh?" But Sarah denied it and said that she did not laugh because she was afraid. Then the Lord said, "Nothing is too hard for the Lord, and you will be with a son when I return the next time." Then the men left.

Sarah conceived and gave birth to Abraham's son in his old age at the set time, as God had promised her. Abraham called the name of his son Isaac. Abraham was one hundred years old when his son Isaac was born.

After all these things, one day God tempted Abraham. Take your only son, Isaac, whom you love very much, and go to the land of Moriah and offer him there a burnt offering upon one of the mountains that I will tell you. Without opposing, the next day Abraham rose early in the morning, saddled his ass, and took Isaac, his son, and two of his young men along with him. He took wood for the burnt offering and went to the place where God told him. On the third day, Abraham saw the place far away. He told his young men: "Stay here with the ass." I will go with the lad yonder (*the indicated place*) and worship and come back again.

Abraham took the wood for the burnt offering, laid it upon his son Isaac, took the fire in his hand and the knife, and both went together. Then Isaac said to his father, "We have the fire and the wood, but where is the lamb for the burnt offering?" Then Abraham said, "My son, God will provide a lamb for the burnt offering." They continued their journey.

Finally, Abraham and his son reached the destination that God had told them about. Abraham built an altar there and laid the wood in order. Then he bound his son and laid him on the altar, upon the wood. Isaac did not resist at all. Abraham then stretched forth his hand and took the knife to slay his son. The angel of the Lord called out of heaven and said, Abraham, Abraham, and Abraham said, "Here am I." The angel said, "Lay not your hand upon the lad, and do not do anything unto him." Now I know you fear God because you offered your only son as an offering.

When Abraham looked up, he saw a ram entangled in the thick thorns. Abraham took the ram and offered the ram as a burnt offering in place of his son. He called that place Jehovah-Jireh, as it is called to this day.

The Angel of the Lord called Abraham out of heaven the second time and said, "Because you have not withheld your only son, I will bless you and multiply your seed like the stars of the heaven and as the sand that is upon the sea shore. Because you have obeyed my voice, all the nations of the earth will be blessed through your seed. Abraham went back to his young men, and they all went to Beer-Sheba.

Sarah died in Kirjath-Arba when she was one hundred and twenty-seven years old. Abraham buried Sarah in the cave of the field of Machpelah before Mamre. It was for the possession of a burial place. Abraham mourned and wept for Sarah.

4. ISAAC MEETS WIFE REBEKAH

Abraham was old and well-stricken in age, and the Lord had blessed Abraham in all things. Abraham said to his eldest servant of his house, who ruled over all that he had, not to take a wife for his son Isaac from the daughters of Canaanites. He also told his servant to go to Abraham's country, where his relatives lived, and take a wife for his son. His servant asked Abraham, "What If the woman was not willing to come to this land?"

Then Abraham said, "The Lord God of heaven, who swore unto me to give this land, will send his angel before you.

Abraham's servant rode ten of his master's camels to Mesopotamia with all the necessary goods. In the evening, he made his camel kneel by a well of water and prayed. Lord, show kindness towards my master Abraham. When the daughters of this city come to draw water, the damsel to whom I shall say, "I may drink," she should let down her pitcher and shall say, "Drink, and I will give your camels also water." Then I will know you have shown kindness to my master, and the same damsel will be Isaac's wife.

As soon as he finished praying, Rebekah came with her pitcher upon her shoulder, who was related to Nahor, Abraham's brother. The damsel was very fair to look at and not married. She went down to the well, filled the pitcher with water, and came back. Abraham's servant ran to meet her and requested some water to drink. She let down her pitcher and gave him a drink, and she offered to draw water for all his camels as well. After the camels had finished drinking water, Abraham's servant took a golden earring and two bracelets and gave them to Rebekah.

The servant asked Rebekah, whose daughter, are you? Rebekah revealed that she was Bethuel's daughter, related to Nahor. He asked her if there was room in her father's house for them to lodge in. She said they had both rooms and enough straw and provender (*food for animals*). He then bowed and worshipped God for leading him to the house of his master's brother.

The damsel ran and told all these things in her house. Then her brother Laban saw the earrings and bracelets on his sister and asked her, "Who had given her all these jewels?" After hearing what his sister told him, he ran out to meet Abraham's servant. He saw the servant standing with the camels at the well. Laban told the servant that he had prepared the house and room for camels. Abraham's servant was given water to wash his feet, straw, and provender for his camels. When food was set before him, he told them he would not eat until he explained the purpose of his visit. The rest all happened according to the prayer that I had made at the well.

Laban said this proceeded from the Lord. Behold, Rebekah is before you; take her and let her be your master's son's wife. After hearing this, Abraham's servant bowed and worshipped the Lord. He then brought jewels of silver, gold, and raiment (clothing), and gave them to Rebekah, he also gave her brother and mother precious gifts.

They all dined together, and the servant and his men tarried (*stayed*) that night. He rose early in the morning and told Laban's family to send him to his master, Abraham. Then Laban and his mother said, "Let Rebekah stay with us for ten days." The servant said, "Do not stop me, for the Lord has prospered my way; send me to my master." Laban and his mother asked Rebekah, if she was willing to go with this man, and she said she would go. Then they sent Rebekah and her nurse, along with Abraham's servant and his men. Rebekah's family blessed her and said, "Be the mother of thousands of millions." Rebekah, along with her nurse, followed the man and rode on the camels.

Isaac went to the field in the evening to meditate. When he lifted his eyes, he saw the camels coming. As soon as Rebekah saw Isaac, she got off the camel. She asked the servant who was the man coming to meet them. Then the servant said, "He is Isaac, my master." Hearing this, Rebekah took a veil and covered herself. The servant narrated all the things that happened. Rebekah became Isaac's wife when he was forty years old. Isaac loved her and was comforted after his mother's death. All the days of Abraham were one hundred and seventy-five years. He was laid to rest next to his wife, Sarah.

5. THE TWINS ESAU AND JACOB

God blessed Isaac after his father Abraham died, and Isaac dwelt by the well Lahairoi. Isaac's wife, Rebekah, was barren (*unable to conceive*), so Isaac prayed to the Lord. Then Rebekah conceived, and the children struggled within her. Then the Lord said unto her, "Two nations are in your womb, and two manners of people shall be separated from your bowels." One shall be stronger than the other, and the elder shall serve the younger. The time for delivery had come, and Rebekah had twins. The first came out red, and he had hair all over his body, and they called him Esau. Then came out his brother, and his hand took hold of Esau's heel, and he was called Jacob. Isaac was sixty years old when his sons Esau and Jacob were born.

The boys grew up. Esau was a smart hunter and took care of the field, but his brother Jacob was a plain man. Isaac loved Esau because he ate the meat of the animals his son hunted and brought home, but Rebekah loved Jacob. One day, when Jacob was cooking pottage (*soup or stew*), Esau came from the field tired, and he said, "I'm going to die of hunger," so give me some pottage. Jacob told Esau, "Sell me your birthright in exchange for the pottage." Esau said, "When I am dying of hunger, what profit do I gain by keeping the birthright?" So Jacob gave Esau bread and a pottage of lentils and took the birthright. Esau ate and went on his way, despising his birthright.

Then there came a famine in the land. So, Isaac went to Abimelech, the King of the Philistines, in Gerar. The Lord appeared to Isaac and told him, "Do not go to Egypt, but dwell in the land that I shall tell you." Sojourn (*stay temporarily*) here, and I will bless you and be with you and your seed. I will perform the oath that I swore to Abraham, your father, and I will multiply your seed like the stars of heaven. These countries I will give to your seed, and all the nations of the earth will be blessed because Abraham obeyed my voice and followed my commandments and my laws.

In the same year, Isaac sowed in that land and received a hundred-fold return, and the Lord blessed him. He had possession of flocks, herds, and a great store of servants, which the Philistines envied. All the wells that his father's servants had dug in the days of Abraham were filled with earth by the Philistines. King Abimelech told Isaac, "You go from us, since you are mightier than us." So Isaac departed from there, pitched his tent, and dwelt in the valley of Gerar. Isaac dug the wells again, which the Philistines had closed after the death of Abraham, and retained the names that his father had kept.

Abimelech went to meet Isaac along with his friend Ahuzzath and Phichol, the chief captain of his army. Isaac told them, "You hated me and sent me away; then why did you come?" Then they said to Isaac, "The Lord is with you." And promise that you will not hurt us, as we have not touched you but have only done good to you and sent you in peace because you are the blessed of the Lord. Isaac made a feast for Abimelech and his men. They dined, rose early in the morning, and departed in peace.

When Isaac grew old and his eyes were dim, he called Esau his eldest son and told him that his days were numbered. Therefore, take your quiver (*container for arrows*) and bow and go to the field and bring me some venison (the meat of a wild animal). Then make me savoury (*tasty*) meat, like the way I love it, and bring it to me so that my soul may bless you before I die. When Rebekah overheard Isaac speaking to Esau, she told Jacob, "Your father said to Esau, "Cook and bring the savoury of your venison for me to eat, and I will bless you before I die."

Hence, Rebekah commanded Jacob "to go to the flock and fetch good kids of goat," and I will make of them savoury meat as your father likes. You go and give the same to your father, that he may eat and bless you. Jacob told his mother, "My brother is a hairy man, but I am a smooth man." My father will feel me, and I will become a deceiver. I will bring a curse upon myself and not a blessing. Then his mother told Jacob, "Let the curse be upon me; you only obey my voice."

Jacob obeyed his mother's command and went to fetch goat kids from their flock. She prepared savoury meat for his father, who adored it. Then Rebekah took the good clothes of her eldest son, Esau, and put them on Jacob, her younger son. She wrapped the skins of the goat kid around Jacob's hands and smooth neck before sending him to Isaac with the savoury meat and bread she had prepared. Jacob approached his father and addressed him as "my father." "Who are you, my son?" Isaac responded. Jacob introduced himself as Esau, "your firstborn son." I have brought the savoury meat; sit and eat my venison, that your soul may bless me.

Isaac asked his son, "How is it that you have found the venison so quickly?" "The Lord, your God, brought it to me," Jacob said. Out of doubt, Isaac said to Jacob, "Come near so I can feel you," whether you are Esau or not. Jacob approached his father, and Isaac felt him. Then Isaac said, "The voice is like Jacob, but the hands are like Esau." Isaac was convinced because his hands were covered in hair. Isaac asked, "Are you my very son, Esau?" And Jacob replied, "Yes, I am." Isaac told him to bring the savoury, and he ate. But Isaac still had doubts. Isaac said, "Come near now and kiss me, my son." Jacob approached his father and kissed him. Isaac smelled the smell of his raiment and blessed Jacob, telling him, "The smell of my son is of a field which the Lord has blessed." God will give you the dew of heaven, the fatness of the earth, and plenty of corn and wine. Let people serve you, and nations bow down to you. You will be Lord over your brother. Blessed be he who blesses you, and cursed be he who curses you.

Jacob went out scared as soon as Isaac finished blessing him. At the same time, Esau came in from his hunting with the savoury meat that he had prepared. Esau told his father, "Arise, eat the venison that I brought, and let your soul bless me." Then Isaac asked, "Who are you?" Esau replied, I am your firstborn son. Isaac was astonished and said, "Who?" Where is he who brought the venison? I have eaten all that he brought before you came. I have blessed him, and he shall be blessed.

When Esau heard the words of his father, he cried bitterly and said, "Oh, my father, bless me also." Isaac said, "Your brother has taken away your blessings cunningly. Esau said, Jacob has supplanted (*replaced*) me twice by taking away my birthright and blessing. Esau asked his father, "Have you not reserved one blessing for me? Isaac answered, I have made him your Lord, and all his brothers I have given him as servants, and I have blessed him with corn and wine; what shall I do to you, my son?

Esau said unto his father, "Have you only one blessing? Bless me also, oh my father." After saying this, Esau lifted his voice and wept. Then Isaac said to Esau, "Your dwelling place shall be the fatness of the earth and the dew of heaven from above." You shall live by your sword and will serve your brother. Esau hated his brother Jacob because he cheated and took away the blessing from their father.

6. JACOB IN PADANARAM

Esau said, I will slay my brother after my father's death. When Rebekah heard this, she wanted to protect Jacob from Esau and devised a plan. Rebekah loved Jacob, so she feared for his life and wanted to protect both her sons. She called Jacob and told him, "My son, obey my voice and go to Laban, my brother, who is in Haran." Stay there with your uncle for a few days, until your brother Esau's anger reduces and he forgets what you have done to him; then I will fetch you from Haran. Rebecca said to Isaac, I do not want the daughters of Heth to be Jacob's wife.

Isaac called Jacob and told him not to take a wife from the daughters of Canaan. Go to your mother's father in Padanaram and take a wife from the daughters of your uncle Laban. The God almighty will bless you, make you fruitful and multiply, and give you the blessing of Abraham. You will inherit the land where you are a stranger, which God gave to Abraham. Then Jacob obeyed their parent's advice and went to his uncle Laban in Padanaram. Esau also, did not take the daughters of Canaan to be his wife because it did not, please Isaac.

Jacob left Beer-Sheba and went towards Haran. Since the sun had set, he wanted to rest a while before he could continue his journey. He took some stones from that place and put them as pillows, then laid down in that place to sleep. While sleeping, he dreamed of a ladder set on the earth. The top of the ladder reached heaven, and he saw the Angels of God ascending and descending on it. The Lord stood above it and said, I am the Lord God of Abraham and Isaac, your father. The land where you lie, I will give you and your seed. Your seed shall be as the dust of the earth, and it shall be spread throughout the east, west, north, and south. All the families of the earth will be blessed through you and your seed. I will be with you wherever you go and will bring you again to this land, for I will not leave you until I have fulfilled what I have promised. Then Jacob woke up afraid from his sleep. He said, "This place is the house of God, and this is the gate of heaven."

Jacob rose early in the morning and took the stones that he had used as pillows and set them up as a pillar, and he poured oil on top of them. He called the name of that place Bethel, but it was called Luz at first. Jacob vowed that if God will be with me on my way that I go, give me bread to eat and clothing to put on, and I come again to my father's house in peace, then the pillar which I have set shall be God's house, and I will surely give the tenth to you.

As he continued his journey into the land of the people of the East, he found flocks of sheep lying by the well in the field, and a great stone was upon the well's mouth. Besides that, three flocks of sheep were gathered near the well, for out of that well they watered the flocks. And a great stone was upon the well’s mouth.

Close-by this well, flocks of sheep were gathered, and the people rolled the stone from the well's mouth, watered the sheep, and put the stone again upon the well's mouth. Jacob inquired of the men who were there around, brother, where are you from? “They said from Haran.” Jacob asked if they knew Laban. They said they knew him. Jacob asked if he was well. They replied that he was well, and behold, his daughter Rachel comes with her father's sheep. When Jacob told the men to water the sheep, they said, "We cannot until all the flocks are gathered."

By then, Rachel had come with her father's sheep. When Jacob saw Rachel, he went and rolled the stone from the well's mouth and watered the flocks of Laban. Jacob was so excited and happy to see Rachel, whom he saw for the first time. So, he went and kissed Rachel, lifted up his voice, and wept. Then Jacob identified himself as Rebekah's son, the sister of your father Laban. Hearing this, Rachel ran and told her father. After hearing this, Laban ran to meet Jacob. Laban embraced Jacob, kissed him, and brought him to his house.

Laban told Jacob, "You are my bone and flesh." Jacob stayed with his uncle for a month. Laban said that though you are my relative, you need not serve me free of cost; what wages do you expect? Laban had two daughters; the elder's name was Leah, and the younger was Rachel. Rachel was more beautiful than her sister Leah, and Jacob liked Rachel. Jacob told Laban that he would serve seven years and marry Rachel. Laban felt it was better to give his daughter to Jacob as his wife than to any other man.

Jacob served seven years for Rachel, and it seemed like a few days to him, for the affection he had towards her was great. Then Jacob told Laban that he would like to marry Rachel. Then a feast was arranged for all the people in the evening. In the evening, Laban brought his daughter Leah and gave her to Jacob to be his wife. Laban gave Zilpah, his maid, to Leah as her handmaid. Only in the morning did Jacob realize that it was Leah and not Rachel. Jacob asked Laban, "Why did you deceive me by giving Leah instead of Rachel?" Then Laban told Jacob that in our country we cannot give the younger daughter in marriage before the elder: "Serve another seven years; I will give you Rachel also as your wife." Jacob had to wait another seven years to marry Rachel. Laban gave Bilhah, his maid, to Rachel as her handmaid.

The names of Jacob's sons were Reuben, the firstborn, then Simeon, Levi, Judah, Issachar, Zebulun, Dan, Naphtali, Gad, Asher, and Joseph. The name of his only daughter was Dinah, and she was the seventh child of Leah. Rachel had one son, and his name was Joseph. After Joseph was born, Jacob told his uncle Laban, "Send me away along with my wives and children that I may go to my place and my country. Laban told Jacob, "Stay here, for the Lord has blessed me because of you; I will give you the wages that you demand."

Jacob told Laban, "You know how I have served you." You had very little cattle before I came to you, but now it has increased abundantly. The Lord has blessed you since I came, but when will I earn money and take care of my family? Jacob had an understanding with Laban that some of the cattle that he took care of for Laban would be his. The Lord had lavishly blessed Jacob with vast herds of cattle, maidservants and male servants, camels, and asses.

One day Jacob heard Laban's sons saying, "Jacob has taken away everything our father had." Jacob's feelings for Laban were no longer the same after this. And the Lord said to Jacob, "Return to the land of your father and your kindred; I will be with you." Jacob called his wives, Leah and Rachel, to the field and said unto them, "Your father's behaviour towards me is not the same as before," but the Lord has been with me. I had served your father with all my heart, but your father deceived me and changed my wages ten times. But God did not allow your father to hurt me. Rachel and Leah asked Jacob, "Is there any portion of inheritance for us from our father?" He has sold us and cheated us out of our money, so do as the Lord have said unto you.

Jacob rose the next day, set his sons and wives upon camels, and carried all his cattle and goods to go to Isaac, his father, in the land of Canaan. Jacob left Padanaram without telling Laban when he had gone to shear (*remove the fleece or hair*) his sheep.

Laban came to know that Jacob had fled on the third day. So, Laban took his brother along with him and pursued Jacob. It took seven days to reach Mount Gilead and overtake Jacob. That night, God appeared to Laban and said unto him, "Speak not anything good or bad to Jacob."

Laban asked Jacob, "Why did you flee secretly with my daughters without telling me?" I would have sent you off with a big farewell. You did a foolish thing by not letting me kiss my children and say goodbye to them. I have the power to hurt you, but the God of your father spoke to me last night and told me not to say anything good or bad to you.

Jacob said, I did not tell you because I was afraid you would take your daughters from me by force. He told Laban, I have been in your house for twenty years. I worked for your two daughters for fourteen years and your cattle for six years out of those twenty years. At times, the cattle were torn in the field by beasts, for which I bear the loss. In the daytime, drought (*dry heat*) consumed me, and the frost by night. It has been a long time since I had proper sleep. The God of Abraham and the fear of Isaac were with me; otherwise, you would have sent me empty. God has seen my distress and warned you last night. They made a covenant (*agreement*) and made a heap of stones as a pillar, and Jacob named that place Galeed. They promised not to pass over this heap to harm each other; the God of our father is the witness between us. They ate and stayed together that night. Early in the morning, Laban woke up, kissed his daughters and grandchildren, and departed for his place.

Jacob left as well to meet Esau, his brother, who was in the land of Seir, the country of Edom. He sent messengers before him to Esau. He told them to tell Esau that your brother Jacob lived with Laban until now and is coming to meet you, and he might find grace in your sight. The Lord has blessed him with oxen, asses, flocks, menservants, and women servants.

The messengers returned to Jacob and told him that your brother Esau was also coming to meet you with four hundred men. Hearing this, Jacob was greatly afraid and distressed, and he divided the people, flocks, herds, and camels into two bands, thinking that if Esau smote (*killed*) one company, at least the other company would escape. Jacob prayed, Lord, you had told me to return to my kindred (*close relatives*), and though I am not worthy of all the mercies that you have shown me, please deliver me from the hand of my brother. I fear that he will come and smite me, my wives, and my children, for you have told me that I will be blessed as the sand of the sea.

Jacob lodged in Jordan that night. The next day, he took whatever was in his hand as a gift for his brother Esau. They were two hundred she goats, twenty he-goats, two hundred ewes, twenty rams, thirty milch camels with their colts, forty kine, ten bulls, twenty she asses, and ten foals. He sent all these into the hands of his servants to be delivered to Esau. Jacob divided the people, the flocks, herds, and camels into two bands. Because if Esau smite one company, the other company will escape. He told them to maintain space between each drive. Jacob told the first band, "If my brother asks you, "Who are these and where are you going?", then you shall say, "All these are presents sent to my Lord Esau." You will also say that your brother Jacob is behind us to make peace with you if you are ready to accept him.

That night Jacob took his two wives, his two female servants, and his children and crossed the stream Jabbok. When Jacob was left alone, a man wrestled with him until the breaking of the day. The man asked, "What is your name? He told Jacob." Then the man told him, "Henceforth, you will not be called Jacob but Israel, because you have power as a prince." He blessed Jacob there. Jacob called the name of that place Peniel because he saw God there.

When Jacob lifted his eyes and looked, he saw Esau coming with his four hundred men. Jacob divided the children among Leah, Rachel, and the two handmaids. He put the handmaids first, then Leah and her children, and in last place he put Rachel and Joseph. Jacob went before them and bowed himself to the ground seven times until he came near his brother. Esau ran and embraced his brother. He fell on Jacob's neck and kissed him, and they both wept.

Esau looked up and saw the women and children and asked, "Who are those with you?" Jacob said that they were the children that God had graciously given to him. First came the handmaids with their children and bowed themselves; then Leah came with her children and bowed themselves; and later Rachel came with Joseph and bowed themselves. Esau asked, "Why did you send those droves that I met?" Jacob said that was to find grace in your sight. Esau said, "Brother, I have enough; you keep what is yours." But Jacob told his brother, "If I have found grace in your sight, receive my present." After I saw you, I felt I had seen the face of God and that you were pleased to see me. Take the present, because God has blessed me, and I have enough. Saying this, he urged his brother to take the gifts, which he did.

Esau returned to Seir, and Jacob went to Succoth. Jacob built a house there and made booths for his cattle. Then Jacob went to Shalem, a city in Shechem, which is in Canaan. He bought a piece of land there and pitched his tent. He erected an altar and called the place Elelochelsrael.

7. JOSEPH'S DREAM

God said to Jacob, "Arise, go to Bethel, and dwell there." Then Jacob did as God had instructed him and went to Bethel with all the people that were with him. Then Jacob went to Luz, in Canaan, and he built an altar there and called the place Elbethel, because God appeared to him when he fled from the face of his brother. Rebekah's nurse, Deborah, died, and she was buried in Bethel. God appeared again unto Jacob and said unto him, "Thy name shall not be called any more Jacob, but Israel shall be your name. God said to be fruitful and multiply, for Kings shall be born from your seed.

When they were on their way to Ephrath, Rachel was in hard labour. The midwife told Rachel that you will have this one, too, a son. While her soul was departing, before she died, she named her son Benoni, but Jacob named him Benjamin. Jacob set a pillar upon her grave, which is the pillar of Rachel's grave to this day. In all, Jacob had twelve sons and one daughter.

Jacob went to his father Isaac, who lived in Hebron. Isaac lived for one hundred and eighty years and gave up the ghost. He was gathered to his people, and his sons Esau and Jacob buried him. Esau and Jacob's riches and cattle were more than they could dwell on together, and the land wherein they were strangers could not bear them. Esau dwelt in mount Seir in the land of Edom. Esau was called the father of the Edomites; dukes were born out of Esau's generation, and they took possession of the land according to their habitation.

Jacob dwelt in the land of Canaan with his children, where his father was a stranger. Jacob's children are Reuben, Simeon, Levi, Judah, Issachar, Zebulun, Dan, Dinah, Naphtali, Gad, Asher, Joseph, and Benjamin. Israel loved Joseph more than all his children because he was the son of his old age. He gave Joseph a special coat of many colours. When Joseph's brothers saw that their father loved him more than the other sons, they hated him. Joseph was seventeen years old and was feeding the flock along with his brothers in the field. Joseph brought all the evil reports of his brothers to his father.

One day Joseph dreamed a dream and told his brothers, and they hated him yet more. Joseph told them, "We were binding sheaves (*grains bound together*) in the field. My sheaf arose and stood upright, and your sheaves stood round about and made obeisance (*bow down*) to my sheaf. Then his brothers asked, "Shall you reign over us or have dominion over us?" They hated Joseph more for his dreams and his words. Joseph dreamed another dream and told his brothers and father. Behold, the sun, moon, and eleven stars made obeisance to me. But his father rebuked him and said, "Shall I, your mother, and brothers bow down to you?" Though his brothers envied him, his father observed the saying.

Joseph's brothers went to feed their father's flock in Shechem. Israel told Joseph to go and find out if his brothers and the flocks were well. When Joseph reached Shechem, a certain man found him wandering in the field and asked Joseph, "What are you searching for?" Then Joseph said he was searching for his brothers, who were feeding their flocks. The man said he heard them say they were planning to go to Dotham. Joseph went after them and found them in Dotham.

When his brothers saw Joseph from far off, they conspired to slay him. They said to one another, "The dreamer comes; let us slay him and cast him into some pit." We'll say an evil beast devoured him, and then we'll see what happens to his dreams. Then Reuben, the eldest of all, said, "Let us not kill him; shed no blood; but cast him into the pit that is in the wilderness." Reuben protected Joseph so that he could deliver him to his father again.

When Joseph came and met his brothers, they stripped him of his coat of many colours and cast him into an empty pit, which did not have any water in it. When Joseph's brothers sat down to eat, they saw a company of Ishmaelites coming from Gilead with their camels, who were going to Egypt. Then Judah said to his brothers, "We do not profit by slaying our brother." Let us sell him to the Ishmaelites without slaying him, for he is our brother and our flesh, and his brothers were content with this decision. They drew Joseph out of the pit and sold him to the Ishmaelites for twenty pieces of silver. The Ishmaelites brought Joseph into Egypt.

When Reuben returned to the pit, he found Joseph missing from the pit. Reuben tore his clothes out of panic and was worried. He came to his brothers and told them that Joseph was missing from the pit; where shall I go and find him? Then they killed a kid of a goat, took Joseph's multicoloured coat, and dipped it in the blood. The brothers sent the blood-stained, multicoloured coat to their father. Israel identified it and said, "It is my son's coat; an evil beast has devoured (destroyed) him, and no doubt he is rent to pieces." Then Jacob tore his clothes and put sackcloth on himself, and he mourned for his son for many days. Though the rest of his children tried to comfort him, he refused to accept that Joseph was no more. He said, "Let me go down to the grave" with my son in mourning, and he wept for him.

8 JOSEPH THE OVERSEER IN EGYPT

The Midianites sold Joseph in Egypt to Potiphar, an officer of Pharaoh. The Lord was with Joseph, and he was a prosperous man who lived in the house of his master, the Egyptian. Joseph's master saw that the Lord was with Joseph, and all that Joseph did, the Lord made it prosper. Joseph found grace in the eyes of his master. He made Joseph the overseer of the house and gave him complete control and responsibility; all that he had he put into Joseph's hands. The Lord blessed the Egyptian's house for the sake of Joseph, and the blessing of the Lord was upon all that he had in the house and in the field. Except the bread that he ate, his master did not know anything in the house.

Joseph was attractive, had a good appearance, and was well liked by everyone. His master's wife cast an eye on Joseph, for she desired him, which he did not give in to. Joseph told his master's wife, "My master has not kept anything from me; I cannot sin against God." One day, when Joseph went into the house to do his usual work and there were no men in the house, his master's wife caught him by his garment. But Joseph fled from his master's wife, leaving the garment behind. She kept the garment with her until her husband came home. After her husband came, she told him that the Hebrew servant whom you had brought misbehaved with me. When I lifted my voice and cried, he left his garment with me and fled out.

As soon as Pharaoh heard the words of his wife about Joseph, his anger kindled (*arose*). He then put Joseph in the prison where the king's prisoners were bound. But the Lord was with Joseph and showed mercy, and Joseph received favour from the keeper of the prison. The keeper of the prison handed over all the other prisoners under the control of Joseph. The other prisoners did what Joseph instructed them to do. The keeper of the prison did not inquire about any activity that Joseph did, because whatever Joseph did, the Lord made it prosper.

After all these things, it so happened that the king of Egypt was wroth (*angry*) with the chief butler and the chief baker because they offended the king. So, the King put both the chief butler and baker in the house of prison where Joseph was bound. The butler and the baker were in prison for some time.

One day both the butler and the baker had a dream in the same night. Each of them dreamed according to their interpretation. When Joseph came in the morning and looked at them, they were sad. Joseph asked them, "Why are you looking sad?" They said to him, "We both had a dream, but there is no interpreter." Joseph urged them to share their vision. The chief butler told his dream to Joseph. In my dream, I saw a vine with three branches in front of me. The vine was budding with fresh blossoms, and the branches had clusters of grapes. King Pharaoh's cup was in my hand. I plucked the grapes, made juice, filled the cup, and gave the cup to Pharaoh. Joseph then interpreted the dream. The three branches are for three days. Within three days, Pharaoh will restore you to your place as the chief butler. You will deliver Pharaoh's cup in his hand, like in the past when you were his butler. Joseph told the butler, "After everything is well set up with you, think of me by showing kindness, mention me to Pharaoh, and bring me out of this prison. I was indeed stolen out of the land of the Hebrews, and here, for no fault of mine, I am put into the dungeon.

When the chief baker saw that the interpretation of the butler's dream was good, he told Joseph, I also had a dream. In my dream, I had three white baskets on my head. The uppermost basket had all varieties of cooked food, and the birds ate them from my basket, which was upon my head. Joseph interpreted the dream for the chief baker. The three baskets are for three days. Within three days, Pharaoh will hang you on the tree, and the birds will eat your flesh.

It so happened that Pharaoh's birthday was on the third day. He made a feast for all his servants. Pharaoh then remembered the chief butler and the chief baker among his servants. He restored the job of the chief butler to him, and the chief butler gave the cup into Pharaoh's hands. As per Joseph's interpretation the chief baker was hanged by Pharaoh. Though all the interpretations came true, the chief butler did not remember Joseph but forgot him.

After two full years, Pharaoh had a dream, and he was standing by the riverside. There came up out of the river seven well-nourished and fat-fleshed cows, and they grazed in the meadow (*cultivated grassland*). Behind them came seven undernourished and lean-fleshed cows. They stood beside the well-nourished cows on the brink (*bank/edge*) of the river. The seven lean-fleshed cows ate up the seven well-nourished and fat-fleshed cows. The lean-fleshed cows still looked unfavourable even after eating the fat-fleshed cows. After the dream, King Pharaoh woke up from his sleep.

Pharaoh went back to sleep and had a second dream the same night. Seven strong and good-quality ears of corn grew and came from one stalk (*stem*). Then seven thin ears of corn that were leafless and blasted by the wind sprung up. The seven thin and blasted ears of corn devoured the strong and good-quality ears of corn. Pharaoh woke up from his sleep and found it to be a dream.

In the morning, Pharaoh's soul was disturbed because of the dream. He sent forth and called for all the magicians and wise men of Egypt. He told them the dream, but none of them were able to interpret the dream of Pharaoh. Then the chief butler told Pharaoh, I realize my mistake today. When you were angry with your servants and put me and the chief baker in prison, we had a dream one night. At that time there was a young Hebrew man, servant to the captain of the guard. We told him about our dreams, and he interpreted them for each of us. As per his interpretation, my job was restored, and the baker was hanged.

Then Pharaoh sent for Joseph, and they brought him out of the dungeon. Joseph shaved and changed his clothes and came to meet Pharaoh. Pharaoh told Joseph, I had a dream, and there is no one to interpret it. I heard that you can understand a dream to interpret it. "It is not I," Joseph told Pharaoh, "but God will give Pharaoh the answer of peace." Pharaoh told both his dreams to Joseph. Joseph informed Pharaoh that both dreams were the same. God has shown Pharaoh what he is going to do.

The seven fat cows and the seven good-quality ears of corn are seven years of great yield. The seven lean cows and the seven blasted ears of corn will be seven years of famine. In the first seven years, there will be plenty of yield throughout all of Egypt. After the first seven years, there shall arise seven years of famine, wherein all plenty shall be forgotten and the famine shall consume the land and be grievous. This is established by God, and God will make it happen shortly.

Joseph told Pharaoh to look for someone who is intelligent and wise and put him in charge over the land of Egypt. Appoint officers over the land, and buy the fifth part of the growth in the land of Egypt in the seven plenteous years. Let the officers gather the food from the first seven good years that come and keep it under the care of Pharaoh in the cities. The food stored will be consumed during the seven years of famine so that the land of Egypt will not perish because of famine. This pleased Pharaoh and his servants.

Then Pharaoh said to his servants, "Can we find anyone other than Joseph in whom the spirit of God is there?" He said unto Joseph, "Since God has shown you all these, there is none so intelligent and wise other than you. You will be the governor of my palace and rule all my people. Only on the throne will I be greater than you.

Pharaoh said unto Joseph, I have made you head over all the land of Egypt. And Pharaoh took off the ring from his hand and put it on Joseph's hand; he dressed him in fine and expensive linen, and he put a gold chain around his neck. He made Joseph ride in the second chariot that he had, and the people bowed down to the new ruler over the land of Egypt. Pharaoh told Joseph, I am Pharaoh, the king, but without your consent, no man shall lift his hand or foot in all the land of Egypt.

9. JOSEPH'S DREAM COME TRUE

Pharaoh gave Joseph Asenath, the daughter of Potipherah, the priest, to be his wife. Joseph was thirty years old. Joseph went out to have a look throughout all the land of Egypt. In the first seven years, the earth brought forth plenty of yield. He gathered all the food from the yield for the first seven years and stored it in the cities in the land of Egypt. He gathered corn like the sand of the sea, until he could not number them.

Before the famine, Joseph had two sons. He named his first child Manasseh because God made him forget his father's house and all the toil that he went through. He named his second son Ephraim, for the Lord had made him fruitful in the land of Egypt during his affliction (*distress or suffering from pain*).

Then the seven years of plenty came to an end in the land of Egypt. The seven years of dearth (scarcity) began, as Joseph had interpreted. Except in Egypt, where food was available, scarcity had spread in all the other lands.

When the people of Egypt were famished for food, they cried and approached Pharaoh for food. Pharaoh said to the Egyptians, "Go to Joseph and do whatever he says unto you." The famine was sore and prevailed all over the face of the earth. Then Joseph opened all the storehouses and sold food to the

Egyptians. All the countries came into Egypt to purchase food from Joseph.

Joseph's father, Jacob, heard that there was food available in Egypt. He told his sons, "Why do you look upon each other's face?". Go to Egypt, where food is available, and get us some food from there so that we may live and not die. Joseph's ten brothers went to Egypt to buy food. But Jacob did not send Benjamin, Joseph's brother, along with the others. He did not want any mischief to befall Benjamin.

The sons of Israel were among those who came to buy food from Egypt because of the famine in Canaan. Joseph was the governor over the land of Egypt, and he was the one who sold food to the people. Joseph's brothers came and bowed themselves before him with their faces to the earth. On seeing his brothers, Joseph immediately recognized them, but his brothers could not recognize him. He spoke harshly to them, asking,

"Where are you from?" They said they came from the land of Canaan to buy food.

Joseph then remembered the dreams that he had of them. He said unto them, "You all are spies who have come to spy on this land." They said no, my lord; we servants have come only to purchase food. We are all true men, the sons born to one man, and we are not spies. Joseph told them again, "You are all spies." They said, "We are twelve brothers, the sons of one man in the land of Canaan." The youngest is with our father, and one of our brothers is lost and unable to be found. Then Joseph said unto them, "That is why I told you, you are spies."

Then Joseph told them, I swear by the life of Pharaoh, unless your younger brother comes, you will not go from here. Send one of you and fetch your younger brother; till then, the rest of you will be in prison. Prove your words if there is any truth; otherwise, surely you are all spies. Joseph kept them all together in custody for three days. On the third day,

Joseph told his brothers, "I fear God, and if you are all faithful men, let one of you be in prison, and the rest of you carry corn for your families."

Joseph told his brothers, "Bring your youngest brother unto me; then I will trust whatever you say is true. His brothers said to one another, "We are guilty regarding our brother Joseph. We saw the pain in his soul when he pleaded with us, but we did not hear; therefore, has this distress come upon us". Then Reuben, the eldest of them, said, I told you not to sin against the child, but you did not listen. So now his blood is taking revenge on us.

They did not know that Joseph understood their conversation because he spoke to them through an interpreter. Joseph went aside from them and wept. He came back again and started communicating with them. He took Simeon from among them and bound him in front of their eyes. Joseph commanded his men to fill their sacks with corn, restore every one's money into his sack, and give them provision for the journey. Joseph's brother's asses were loaded with corn, and they departed from there. On the way, one of them opened his sack to give food to his ass and found his money, for it was in his sack's mouth. He told his brothers that his money was restored in his sack. They were worried and afraid. They said to one another, "Why is it that God has done this to us?"

Finally, they came to Jacob, their father, and narrated all that had befallen them. The man, who is the lord of the land, spoke rudely to us and presumed us to be spies of the country. We told him we are twelve brothers, born to one father; one of us is lost, and the youngest is with our father in the land of Canaan. The lord of the country told us, "Leave one of your brothers with me and take food for your families and go." Bring your youngest brother, and then I will know that you are true men and not spies. Then I will deliver your brother, and you can do business in this land.

The brothers emptied their sacks, and each one's bundle of money was in his sack. When they and their father saw the bundles of money, they were afraid. Jacob said unto them, I am already sad because Joseph is not there; now Simeon is not there; and you want to take Benjamin also away. All these things are happening against me. Then Reuben told his father, "Send Benjamin with me; I will bring him back, or else slay my two sons." Jacob said Benjamin will not go with you because his brother is dead and he is left alone. If any mischief befalls him on the way, I will go down to the grave with sorrow.

The food that they brought from Egypt got exhausted. Jacob told his sons to go to Egypt, buy some food, and come, since the famine was sore in the land. Then Judah said unto his father, "The man strictly told us: You shall not see my face, except your brother come with you." We will go and buy food only if you send our brother with us; otherwise, we will not go. Israel asked, "Why did you tell the man you had another brother?" They said that Joseph straightaway asked us about our state and our family. He also asked, "Is your father still alive? And do you have another brother?" We only answered according to the questions he asked. We were surprised when he said, "Bring your younger brother."

Then Judah said to his father, "Send Benjamin with me so that we will go and get food, that we and our little ones may live and not die." You can hand him over to me, and I will take the responsibility. If I do not bring him back, then let me take the blame forever. Had we not lingered here for long, we would have gone and come back the second time.

Their father Israel told them, "If it be so, take the best fruits, a little balm, some honey, spices, myrrh, nuts, and almonds." Also take double the money in your hand, including that which was brought back in the mouth of your sacks the previous time if it was an oversight. Take your brother Benjamin also with you and go unto the man. God Almighty's mercy will be there, so that he may send Simeon and Benjamin.

They took the presents and double the money, and Benjamin went along with them to Egypt and stood before Joseph. When Joseph saw Benjamin with them, he said to the ruler of his house, "Bring these men home and prepare a fat meal." These men will dine with me in the afternoon. The ruler did as Joseph had instructed him. Joseph's brothers were afraid because they were brought into Joseph's house. They thought it was because of the money that was returned in their sacks the first time. He might find an opportunity to find fault and take us prisoners along with our asses.

They came near the steward of Joseph's house and communed with him. They said, "We came here for the first time also to buy food." When we were on our way back home the first time, we opened our sacks and found everyone's money in the mouth of his sack. We have brought that money again with us and have also brought money to buy food this time. We do not know who put the money in our sacks. The steward told them not to fear, for your God and the God of your father had put treasure in your sacks. Then he brought Simeon to them.

The steward brought Benjamin and his brothers into Joseph's house. He gave them water to wash their feet and provender to their asses. They kept the presents ready to give Joseph when they were going to dine with him during lunch time. When Joseph came home, his brothers brought him the presents that were in their hands and bowed themselves to him before the earth. Joseph asked them about their father's well-being and if he was still alive. They answered that their father was doing well and was still alive. Then they bowed their heads and made obeisance.

Joseph then lifted his eyes and saw his brother Benjamin and asked, "Is this your younger brother of whom you were speaking?" He told Benjamin, God be gracious unto you, my son. Joseph's heart was yearning for his brother Benjamin, since both were born to Rachel. Joseph sought a place to weep, so he entered his chamber and wept there. Then he washed his face and went out, controlling himself, and told them to lay the food. Joseph made them sit according to their ages, from the eldest to the youngest. The brothers were surprised at the seating and marvelled (*astonished*) one to another. He shared the food that was kept for him with his brothers. But Benjamin's share was five times more than his brothers. They were merry and enjoyed the togetherness.

Joseph commanded the steward of his house to fill the men's sack with food, as much as they could carry, and put back every one's money in the sack's mouth. Then put my silver cup in the sack's mouth with the youngest and his corn money. The steward did according to what Joseph had commanded. The next day, early in the morning, the men and their asses were sent away.

When they had gone out of the city, but not very far, Joseph said to his steward, "Follow the men and overtake them. Ask them why it is that you have rewarded evil for good. You have taken the silver cup that my lord drinks from." The steward reached the men and asked them why they had taken the silver cup. Then the men said, "Lord, why do you say all these things?" Such things are very far from us. The money that we found in our sacks mouths the first time, we brought back that money this time; how is it that we will steal out of the lord's house? They told him, "In whose ever sack you find the cup, let him die, and we will be my lord's bondmen."

Then they quickly took every man's sack to the ground and opened everyone's sack. The steward started searching the sack from the eldest to the youngest, and the cup was found in Benjamin's sack. They tore their clothes; every man loaded his ass, and they returned to the city. Judah and his brothers came to Joseph's house. Joseph was there in the same place. They fell before Joseph on the ground. Joseph asked them, "What have you done?" Then Judah told, how should we prove ourselves innocent? We are your servants, found guilty in front of you. Then Joseph told them, "In whose hand the cup is found, he shall be my servant, and the rest of you return unto your father in peace."

Judah came near to Joseph and said, "My Lord, just listen to me and let not your anger be against me," for you are equal to Pharaoh. We have followed all your instructions, though our father refused to send our youngest brother Benjamin with us. I had promised my father to take back Benjamin, or else I would take the blame forever. If my father sees that Benjamin is not with us, he will die. So, instead of Benjamin, I beg to remain as a bondman to my lord. How will I return to my father without him? I cannot see the evil that will befall my father.

Joseph could not refrain himself before all of them, so he told all his men to go out of the place. After everyone left, Joseph cried and made himself known to his brothers. He wept so loudly that the Egyptians and all the people in the house of Pharaoh heard. Then he revealed to his brothers that he was Joseph. Is my father still alive? His brothers were shocked and were unable to answer him. He told his brothers to come near him, and they came near him. He said, I am Joseph, your brother, whom you sold in Egypt.

Joseph told them: do not be grieved or angry with yourselves because you sold me. For it was God who sent me here before you to preserve life and to deliver you from the famine. The famine has been going on for two years; there are yet five more years of famine, and there will be neither a yield nor a harvest. So now it was not you that sent me here, but it was God's plan. He had made me a father to Pharaoh, the lord of all his houses, and ruler throughout all the land of Egypt.

Joseph told them, "Go to my father quickly and tell him, your son Joseph is the lord of all Egypt. He has invited you without any delay and told you can dwell in the land of Goshen;

you and your children, your children's children, your folks, your herds—all can be near me. Tell my father all about my glory in Egypt and all that you have seen, and bring my father as fast as possible, because the famine is going to persist for another five years.

He fell upon his brother Benjamin's neck and wept, and Benjamin wept upon Joseph's neck. Joseph kissed all his brothers and wept on each other's shoulders. They had a long conversation and enjoyed each other's company. Everyone in Pharaoh's house came to know about Joseph's brothers. The thing pleased Pharaoh and his servants. Pharaoh told Joseph, tell your brothers to load the asses and go to the land of Canaan and to bring your father and your household. I will give you the best piece of land in Egypt. Take wagons from Egypt for your little ones and wives, and bring your father. Do not worry about your stuff, because the good of all the land of Egypt is yours.

According to Pharaoh's command, Joseph gave his brothers wagons and food to eat on the way. He gave each of them changes of clothing, but to Benjamin he gave three hundred pieces of silver and five changes of clothing. To his father, he sent ten asses laden with the good things of Egypt, ten she asses laden with corn, bread, and meat for his father.

His brothers departed from Egypt. They reached Canaan and told their father Jacob that Joseph was alive and that he was the governor over all the land of Egypt. Hearing this, Jacob's heart fainted because he did not believe them. They told him everything Joseph had said to them. When Jacob saw the wagons that Joseph had sent to carry him, his spirit was revived. Jacob said, I am glad that my son is alive. I will go and see him before I die.

10. JACOB REUNITES WITH SON JOSEPH

After Israel heard that his son Joseph was alive, he started his journey with all that he had and came to Beersheba and offered sacrifices to God. That night God spoke in the vision and said to Jacob, "Fear not to go down to Egypt, because I will make of you a great nation there." I will go down with you into Egypt and will surely bring you out of Egypt. Jacob left Beersheba along with his children, their wives, and the little ones in the wagons that Pharaoh had sent to carry him. They took their cattle and goods, which they had in the land of Canaan, and came to Egypt.

All the souls that came into Egypt, which were Jacob's sons, his sons' wives, his grandson's, and his granddaughter's, were seventy in all, including Joseph, his wife, and his two sons'. Jacob sent Judah before him to Joseph. They came into the land of Goshen. Joseph made ready his chariot and went to meet Jacob, his father, in Goshen. He met his father, fell on his neck, held on to him, and wept for a good while. Then Jacob said to his son, "Now let me die, because you are alive, and I saw your face."

Joseph told his father and brothers, "I will go and tell Pharaoh that my brothers and my father's house have come to me from

Canaan. They have brought their flocks, their herds, and all that they have." When Pharaoh shall call and ask you, "What is your occupation? Then you shall say, we are men of shepherds, and our trade has been to feed cattle since our youth." We and our fathers have been shepherds; allow us to dwell in the land of Goshen, because Egyptians hate shepherds.

Then Joseph came and told Pharaoh my father, my brothers, their flocks, and their herds had come from the land of Canaan to the land of Goshen. Joseph brought five of his brothers and presented them to Pharaoh. Pharaoh asked Joseph's brothers, "What is your occupation? They said that both we and our fathers are shepherds." They requested that Pharaoh allow them to dwell in the land of Goshen because there were no pastures for their flocks and the famine was sore in the land of Canaan, "so we have come here to stay for some time."

Pharaoh told Joseph, "Your family has come to you; the land of Egypt is before you." Make your father dwell in the best of the land of Goshen. If you know anyone who is talented among them, then make them rulers over my cattle. Joseph brought Jacob and set him in front of Pharaoh, and Jacob blessed Pharaoh. Pharaoh asked Jacob, "How old are you? Jacob said he was one hundred and thirty years old." Joseph gave in possession to his father and brothers the best of the land of Egypt, in Remeses, as Pharaoh had commanded. Joseph nourished his father, his brothers, and all his father's household with food according to their families.

There was no food in all the land, because the famine was so severe all over the land of Egypt and all the land of Canaan. Joseph brought to Pharaoh's house all the money that was gathered in the land of Egypt and Canaan, which he obtained from the sale of food. When the money got exhausted from the people of Egypt and Canaan, they came to Joseph and said, "Give us bread; for why should we die in your presence?" If they didn't have money, Joseph told them to give their cattle and take food. So, everyone brought their cattle, horses, flocks, and asses to Joseph in exchange for food for that whole year.

When the year came to an end, they came to Joseph the next year again for food. They said unto him, "My Lord, we have spent all our money; you have our cattle; we have nothing left." We only have our bodies and lands. They begged Joseph, "Buy us and our land for food, or else we would perish before your eyes." We and our land will be servants to Pharaoh. Let the land be used, and we will also be alive. Joseph bought all the land from the Egyptians for Pharaoh. Everyone in Egypt sold his field because the famine prevailed over them, and the land became Pharaoh's. Joseph removed the people from one end of the borders of Egypt and moved them to the other end of the cities. Joseph did not buy the land of the priests because the priests had a portion assigned to them by Pharaoh. The priests ate from the portion that Pharaoh had given them, and they did not sell their lands.

Joseph said unto the people, I have bought the land from you for Pharaoh; you can sow the land with the seed that I have given you. You shall give the fifth part of the yield to Pharaoh, and four parts belong to you. In the four parts, you can sow, and the yield that comes out of it belongs to you. You can feed your little ones and all your households. They told Joseph, "You have saved our lives; let us find grace in the sight of my lord, and we will be Pharaoh's servants."

Jacob and his household lived in the land of Egypt; they had a lot of possessions and multiplied abundantly. When Jacob grew old, he called Joseph his son and made him promise that he should not bury him in the land of Egypt after he died. I would like to be buried with my fathers, so carry me out of Egypt, and Joseph promised to do so.

Joseph came to know that his father was sick, so he took his two sons, Manasseh and

Ephraim, to meet his father. When Jacob was told that his son Joseph was coming, Israel strengthened himself and sat on the bed. When Joseph arrived, Jacob told him that God Almighty appeared to me in Luz, in Canaan, and blessed me. Almighty said, I will make you fruitful and multiply your seed, and I will give this land to your seed for everlasting possession. Your sons, who were born to you in Egypt, are also mine, like Reuben and Simeon. Any children born to you after Manasseh and Ephraim shall be yours, and they will be called after the names of their brothers in their inheritance.

When I came from Padanaram, Rachel, your mother, died in the land of Canaan, on the way to Ephrath. I buried her on the way, which is called Bethlehem. Israel looked at Joseph's sons and asked, "Who are they? Joseph said, they are my sons'." Israel told Joseph to bring his sons closer because Israel's eyes were dim due to old age and he could not see. Joseph brought his sons near his father, who kissed and embraced them.

Israel told Joseph, I did not expect to see your face, but God has shown you and your children as well.

Israel stretched out his hand and kept his right hand on Ephraim's head and his left hand on Manasseh's head to bless them. Joseph tried to remove Israel's right hand from Ephraim's head to Manasseh's head, who was the firstborn. But Israel refused and said, I know it, my son, for the younger brother shall be greater than the elder one, and his seed shall become a multitude of nations. Israel blessed Joseph and told him, I am going to die, but God shall be with you and bring you again to the land of your fathers. Moreover, I have given you one portion of land more than your brothers. Jacob gave a larger portion of land to Joseph because he loved him more than his other sons.

Jacob gathered all his sons and blessed everyone according to their blessing. He told them I am going to be gathered unto my people. Bury me with my fathers in the land of Canaan, which Abraham bought for the possession of a burial place, where Abraham and Sarah his wife, Isaac and Rebekah his wife, and Leah, my wife, are buried. When Jacob made an end of talking to his sons, he gathered up his feet on the bed and gave up the ghost. Jacob lived in the land of Egypt for seventeen years and died when he was one hundred and forty-seven years old.

After Jacob died, Joseph fell on his father's face, wept upon him, and kissed him. Joseph commanded his servants, the physicians, to embalm his father, and they did so. The household of Joseph mourned for Israel for seventy days. After the days of mourning were over, Joseph told Pharaoh, "My father made me swear, saying that I should bury him in the land of Canaan." I would like to go and bury my father, and I will come back. Pharaoh instructed Joseph to carry out his father's wish.

Along with Joseph went both chariots and horsemen. All the household of Joseph went to bury Jacob, except the little ones and their herds and flocks, who were left in the land of Goshen. They came to Atad, which is beyond Jordan, and they mourned there for seven days. Then Jacob's sons carried him into the land of Canaan and buried him in the cave that Abraham had bought for burying. Joseph and his brother returned to Egypt after burying their father.

Joseph's brothers were worried; now that their father was no more, Joseph will hate them and requite (*to return*) them for all the evil that they did to him. They sent a messenger to Joseph to convey what their father had commanded them before he died. Jacob had told them to ask forgiveness from Joseph for all the trespasses (*sins*) they had committed. Hearing this, Joseph wept. Then Joseph's brothers went and bowed themselves before him and told him, "We are your servants." Joseph said, "Fear not; I will not harm you." You thought evil of me, but

God brought me here for a good cause: to save people's lives. He spoke kindly to them: "Therefore, fear not; I will nourish you and your little ones."

Joseph told his brothers, "God will surely bring you out of this land and take you to the land that he swore to Abraham, Isaac, and Jacob, our fathers." He took an oath with his brothers to carry his bones from Egypt after his death. Joseph lived in the land of Egypt for one hundred and ten years and saw Ephraim's children of the third generation. After his death, they embalmed him and put him in a coffin in Egypt.

Thank you for being a part of this Incredible Journey, and we look forward to sharing the next volume 2 with you very soon.

9 798890 660572

Printed by Libri Plureos GmbH in Hamburg, Germany